^AMATTER ^{OF}FAITH

A Memoir of My Spiritual Journey
to the Marian Apparitions in Europe

KATHLEEN HOCTOR–BIELER

SPIDER BOOKS
PUBLISHING

A Matter of Faith

A Memoir of my Spiritual Journey to the Marian Apparitions in Europe

Published by:
Spider Book Publishing
Fort Myers, Florida
SpiderBooksPublishing.com
(239) 693-DRAW

Printed in the United States

ISBN: 978-1-942728-04-7 (print)

ISBN: 978-1-942728-05-4 (digital)

Cover Design by Jennifer Grivens

Interior Design by Jennifer FitzGerald

∞

** To My Blessed Mother **

CONTENTS

∞

PREFACE

God is with us always. He is constantly trying to communicate with us. He loves us as no other can and wants us to feel His presence through every venue. He desires for us to love Him back, by having faith in Him. Faith affirms our love for Him.

In this book, I will attempt to honestly convey the different ways I believe God was trying to communicate with me during this journey. In the following pages, I will endeavor to describe the best I can the 'supernatural' elements of my spiritual experiences.

However, sometimes there are no words in the human language that are capable or appropriate to convey such things as these.

It would be an understatement to say it changed my life. How so? One of the major ways was by increasing my faith in God. In this world we live in today, that is no small feat!

The goal was to see as many Marian apparition sites as I could in a 10-day time constraint. Some of these include 'Our Lady of Fatima, Portugal; the 'Shrine of the Most Holy Miracle' in Santorum, Portugal; St. Bernadette's vision of the Blessed Mother in Lourdes, France, (including her home, the Cachot in Lourdes, France); and on to Lisieux and Carmel, France to visit St. Therese of the Little Flower.

There were several other unusual occurrences that transpired while there, however this memoir will hold only to the above. These alone should attest to the overall theme of this manuscript, which is the importance of having Faith in one's life.

My journey took me to Portugal,

∞

Spain and France. It was from 09/26/12 to 10/06/12. Ten days to explore, experience, and question the presence of God around me, in an incredibly surreal way. Here, I am writing a book about that experience almost 3 yrs. later.

What took me so long? There are a few answers to that question.

First, it is an arduous task to take on, and from the onset I realized I would have to spend many hours alone, dedicated to the book. Next, it took me about a year till I was ready to share my experiences. I spent months trying to make some sense of it all. What did it all mean? Why me? And what was the message that I was supposed to get? I also imagined that by sharing my experiences, it could very well set me up as being a religious quack. So I had to come to terms with all of this before I set out.

Considering these things alone, I put it on the back burner, so to speak, and tried to get

∞

on with my life. Then there was the internal gnawing that kept me up nights, praying for wisdom, discernment and guidance. If the Lord truly wanted me to share this, then I believed He would make it clear to me. The message I received was to just begin writing, and He would serendipitously and synchronistically affirm it, and this He did!

In other words, He put the 'right' people and situations directly in front of me. All I was asked to do was be willing to stay aware and accept the grace that He put before me. Above all, I had to have faith, that if this book was meant to be written, then He would also provide the ways and the means to do so. That meant I needed to 'let go and let God' no matter where that might lead me. I later discovered just how difficult this was going to be!

It entailed me moving my residence from one state to another. Having to sell my home in a very bad market didn't help either, but I tried to stay focused on the guidance and

∞

the goal, and ignore the many frustrations and fears associated with such an endeavor. Besides, I wondered, what did moving have to do with me writing this book? Plenty!

Looking back, I now believe that the good Lord coordinated all the circumstances and opportunities that I needed to begin writing and to stick with it till its completion. I moved from Delaware to Pa., supposedly to be closer to friends and family, however that is not the way it worked out. I moved here to Doylestown in November of 2013. My apartment was small, but had the view from a high rise perspective to be very quiet and conducive to writing.

There started to be strains on my relationships, with both family and friends. This to the point that the relationships were totally changed. Situations occurred that made me feel I had to let the relationships go, at least for the time being. This troubled me immensely, as I thought this was why I was moving back home. I basically ceased

∞

contact with six close relationships all within 1 year. I kept thinking, what is going on? This is not what I had planned on after all. I was very sad and totally confused.

However, all of a sudden, I had the time and space to devote to the writing of this book. I had taken a small part time job when I first moved here, but then suddenly lost that also. So, without a doubt, I now had the time to devote to the book, but will I have the opportunities needed to present this book to others once written?

Yes! I quickly realized that when God affirms something, everything needed for the task is provided. That lesson was another take away.

Doors began to open. The apartment complex that I moved into changed ownership. These folks really wanted to make some well needed changes to the place and then to get the word out that they were here now in the community and they were different!

∞

They held a Christmas Fair that included some 30 vendors from the community, and I decided to be a part of it by having a book signing and sale of my first book, 'Under An Emotive Sky'. It was a grand success!

Afterwards, when the new owners discovered I was a writer of sorts, they asked me if I would be interested in having a single event book signing in the Spring of 2015, and that they would sponsor it for me. They were referring to 'Under An Emotive Sky'. However, I recognized it as an affirming grace to complete and publish 'A Matter Of Faith', by that deadline. I got busy on it immediately!

Amazing! Now I had the time and opportunity to complete 'A 'Matter Of Faith.' I figured God had answered my questions, and to get going on the book. The following pages are not only an account of how God contacted me on my journey, but also about making a declaration of faith by the scary prospect of Letting Go and Letting God...

I pray you are inspired by this reflection, and may you come to know, as I have, that our God is always with us and wants nothing more than to love you and be loved back. For this He will bless you immeasurably! And that my friends is always a Matter Of Faith…

∞

CHAPTER I

THE SHRINE OF THE MIRACLE OF THE HOST

SANTORUM, PORTUGAL

Not far from the Catholic shrine at Fatima (and 45 miles north of Lisbon) is Santorum, Portugal. The home of a 13th-century Eucharistic miracle, which holds the shrine in the Church of the Miracle of the Host, St. Stephen's Church.

It is one of the most famous of its kind and is visited by thousands of pilgrims yearly. The main attraction of the Church of the Miracle of the Host is of course, the Eucharistic Miracle of Santorum, where the Eucharistic Host is enshrined in a brilliant

∞

crystal box that is within a silver monstrance. It is on display atop a multi-tiered tabernacle that is hidden behind a wall and above a ceiling. Other notable interior features of the church are four paintings that depict the miracle, and 16th-century glazed tiles.

SHRINE OF THE MOST HOLY MIRACLE OF SANTAREM

According to the data recorded on the copy of a document commissioned by King

∞

Alfonso IV in 1346, was the following:

On February 16, 1266 at Santorum (in Portugal), a young woman seized with jealousy towards her husband, consulted a sorceress, who advised her to go to Church and steal a consecrated Host in order to make a love potion from it.

The woman stole the Host and hid it in a linen cloth, which at once was stained with Blood. Terrified, she ran to her home, where she opened up the handkerchief to see what happened. With great amazement, she saw that the Blood was gushing from the Host itself. Confused, the woman put the Host in a small drawer in her bedroom, but during the night, beams of light radiated from the drawer, making the room bright as in daylight. Her husband likewise noticed the strange phenomenon and began to question his wife, who then had to tell him the whole story.

The following day, the couple informed

∞

the Pastor, who went to their house and picked up the Host. He took it back to the Church of St. Stephen in solemn procession, followed by many religious and laymen. The Host continued to bleed for three consecutive days. It was then placed in a magnificent reliquary made of bees' wax.

In 1340, another Miracle took place there, when a priest opened the tabernacle and found the waxen vessel broken in pieces, and in its place was a vessel made of crystal, inside of which the Blood of the Host was found mixed with the wax.

Today, the Miraculous Host is preserved in an 18th century monstrance above the main altar, within the wall. The Church of St. Stephen is known as the Shrine of the Holy Miracle. The Host has dripped Blood on several occasions over the centuries, and various images of Our Lord Jesus Christ have been seen to appear in it. Among the testimonies to the Miracle is likewise St. Francis Xavier, the apostle of India, who

∞

visited the Shrine before departing on his mission.

Ever since the occurrence of the Miracle, every year on the second Sunday of April, the precious Relic is carried in procession from the married couple's house to the Church of St. Stephen.

After a very long 8-hour flight, in which I could not sleep a wink, we arrived in Lisbon, Portugal, from Philly. We had to wait for a couple of hours at the Lisbon airport, (which seemed very chaotic). The security there seemed to pay special attention to me, making me dump out my toiletry bag several times, finally instructing me to throw out my bag and buy a clear bag for it all.

After another long wait to get our rental car, we finally hit the road heading north toward our destination, Fatima. There were speed limits there that we pushed to the limit and above, at about 80 to 90 mph, as we were not sure when the different attractions

∞

in Fatima closed up for the day.

In spite of the time constraints we thought we had, we spontaneously decided to make a stop over in the little town of Santorum, Portugal on the way to Fatima. We wanted to see the Shrine of the Miracle of the Host at St. Stephen's Church. We got off at the exit slowly entering the town, and started to look for a place to park. We found one almost immediately and parked.

Then we got out and started to walk in whatever direction we felt led, as we did not plan this, so did not have a map. Once or twice we stopped to ask questions of the local folks, as to where this place was located, but it was not very helpful due to the language barrier. So, we kept walking, deciding to just continue to follow our intuitions (the spirit). My traveling partner had the benefit of 'internal spiritual guides', who proved to be incredibly accurate throughout this journey.

∞

We seemed to be wandering at times, when she would stop a moment and then blurt out, "Ok, we need to turn left or go right". Always, we ended up being right where we had intended to be or sometimes, where we were 'meant' to be. That was often an even more incredible experience!

It wasn't a very big town, so we figured we would eventually find it while meandering around the narrow, hilly cobblestone streets. My friend happened to know a little Spanish and I a little French, but were at a true disadvantage, as neither of us knew Portuguese, but we kept walking just the same. I was the one continually lagging behind my travel buddy, cause I was taking so many pictures, however she was pretty patient and I guess was very used to traveling alone anyway.

Finally, she turned to me and said, I feel like we are close to it. Anyway, we climbed up another narrow hill, and I had to stop a moment to catch my breath, as my atrial

fibulation slowed me down a bit on this journey. When I looked up we were standing right in front of our destination, the Church of the Miracle of the Host, St. Stephens.

I was becoming very impressed with these guides of hers. She walked inside, as I followed closely behind her. That is when I began to feel strange. It was like a low-grade pulsation going through my entire body, almost like it was buzzing, without so much as 1 glass of wine. The old musty smell is what hit my senses next, as we walked in through the mammoth, crusty, wooden doors, many centuries old.

I paused a moment to take it all in, as it was beginning to be a bit overwhelming and I was out of breath. I began clicking away, taking many pictures. The church was indeed breathtaking, but there was something more! Something drew me in closer to the altar. I winded around behind the altar and continued to take pictures. Suddenly, there was a harsh voice in Portuguese directed

∞

toward me. I did not understand his words, but easily recognized the tone as one of anger. He did not want me to take any more pictures. That I was on holy ground! I stopped! My friend was off to the side of the altar, brokering what appeared to be some kind of deal with an old woman, who looked like a church custodian. My friend gestured for me to come over. I was glad to smile politely and walk away from the upset old man. However, he walked over behind me to join up with the old woman and my friend. I think the old man and woman were husband and wife. Amused, I knew he was determined from that point on to keep his eye on me.

When I got there, the old woman tucked the money my friend had given her into her old housedress pocket and then said a few unrecognizable sentences to the old man. Then he took the lead and gestured for us to follow him down a long, narrow hall, toward something he was going to show us. It seemed he was on a mission walking down

∞

that hall, but still kept an eye on my camera and me. I smiled at him again and tucked it away in my pocket, while following the little caravan of four.

We passed some beautiful paintings on the wall, as we walked along. These were not all in frames, but rather painted into the wall, more like murals. I was so tempted to take pictures of these beautiful paintings, but thought better of it. Besides, I was then very curious at that point, as to where he was leading us. I had a sense of mystery of the Sacred almost, as we walked down this long hallway.

He stopped about midway down the hall and turned toward the wall, where there was a little gate in front of a tiny door embedded in the wall. He fumbled with some keys, as I continued to eye the gorgeous paintings surrounding me. He opened the small gate first and then the tiny door that was almost the same size as the gate, about 5 by 3 ft.

∞

He slowly opened it. Inside it was dark, but I could see a tiny, narrow set of about 12 ascending stairs, that ended above where the ceiling was located. So, I was not able to see anything above the point of the ceiling, unless I walked up those stairs.

My friend went first. She slowly took one step, then the next, until she came to a stop. I watched her disappear into the dark ascending hole, to the point where I could only see her legs.

It was almost like a low-lying attic. But right there she stopped and remained for about 5 minutes, obviously looking at something, I could not yet see. She slowly backed down the narrow steps, as there was not enough room where one could turn the body around. It was now my turn to look at whatever it was she had seen at the top of those steps. I was anxious to see whatever it was that left such a pleasant look on her face.

∞

I took a deep breath and climbed up quickly, almost hitting my head where you needed to duck under the ceiling in order to come upon whatever was there. I didn't have a clue as to what I would see, but I was hurrying to see it! Well, as I brought my head up after ducking and barely hitting the ceiling, the pulsating vibrations started again in my body. First in my legs, causing me to hold on tighter to the guardrails on each side of the very narrow stairwell. I was in front of a glass case, which had something in a smaller glass case inside of it. The vibrations continued up through my legs, but now much stronger! I thought maybe I ran up the narrow stairs too quickly.

My eyes were trying their best to focus in on what was in front of me. I could not make it out at first. It was lit from the inside, but the dark surroundings made it difficult at first to understand what I was looking at. When all of a sudden it registered in my mind, what I may have been looking at. At the exact moment that I realized I was

∞

viewing a 'bleeding host', the vibrations shot up my legs and into my throat!

My head was spinning, my eyes blinking through tears. Would I be able to hold on and not fall backward? The vibration then hit my head, and the jolt almost knocked me back down the stairs. I had to hold on to the rails very tightly now because my whole body was shaking! Through it all, I could not take my gaze off of what was in front of me.

Then I was overwhelmed emotionally and the tears began rolling down my face. I believed I was staring at, fixated upon a true miracle.

There before my now wide eyes was the Host/Sacred Heart of Jesus Christ! It was halfway decimated along the edges, with a lining of what appeared to be dried blood. Toward the center of the Host, was a brighter red and it had a pulsating quality to it. I stared deeply into it and that is when

∞

I saw the form of His body conglomerate around His bleeding heart! What was going on here? I could not stop the flow of my tears. Was I staring at Christ, Himself? Could this be real?

I stayed there a long time, in fact, I lost track of time. I spoke internally to Him and as I did, He filled my entire body with warmth and a kind of love so full, that I knew I had never experienced such a love as this, ever in my entire life.

I don't remember coming back down the stairs, but suddenly I was at the bottom and my friend was just staring at me. The old man locked the door and gate up and we were led to the exit. I didn't feel like taking any more pictures in there. My life would never be the same again, and I knew it, and this was just the very beginning of our journey.

We walked to our car in silence, got in and quietly headed north to Fatima. What was

ahead of me I did not know, but thought to myself, what could ever be more mystifying, than what I had just experienced? I could not wait.... but could I handle it? That was the question in my mind. Could I handle it?

CHAPTER II

FATIMA

We arrived in Fatima at about 4:30pm.
We pulled up into the long winding driveway
with the huge 'castle like' structure ahead of

∞

us. The first thing I noticed was the unusual cloud formations in the sky. The sky seemed bigger somehow, and with the odd cloud formations, it appeared almost like a huge easel. The different shapes were taking different forms very quickly. It was almost mesmerizing, but I quickly snapped out of it, to get my luggage out of the car.

Our hotel, the Domus Pacis, meaning House of Peace, is a Guest House and also the headquarters of the International Center of the World Apostolate of Fatima. Domus Pacis is above all, one of the eminent landmarks in the region, famous for the apparitions of Our Lady in 1917.

THE 3 SECRETS OF FATIMA

The First Secret that the 'Beautiful Lady' told the three children of Fatima had to do with the need to amend our ways of the world. They were given a very clear vision of hell, which scared the children tremendously! They related how they saw

the ground split open, spurting voluminous flames of fire!

Within that conflagration they viewed embers of human like souls that were charred and that fell back into the inferno, screaming unrelentlessly! Among the pitiful souls were demons that resembled unknown, translucent, black beings. The vision only lasted for a minute or less and had the 'Beautiful Lady' not warned them ahead of time, they would have fainted away.

In the Second Secret the Blessed Mother told the children that the present war (WWI) would end shortly, but because of the continued grave offenses of men, another war (WWII) would start soon.

Also, She revealed to them that it was God's desire to establish in the world the devotion to Mary's Immaculate Heart. If this devotion was heeded, many souls would be saved and there will be peace. If not, Russia would spread errors throughout the world,

∞

causing wars and persecutions of the church.

The good would be martyred and the Pope would suffer much; various nations will be annihilated! She said that in the end her Immaculate Heart will triumph, and the Pope will consecrate Russia over to Mary and Russia will be converted.

The Third Secret has still not been officially confirmed. Supposedly, Pope John Paul II on 5/13/2000, the 83rd anniversary of the Fatima apparition, released the Vatican's version of the secret. However, what was reported was not in full. The Pope spoke about a major Church apostasy coming down from the highest realms of the Church.

The hotel where we stayed is situated only a few minutes walking distance from Our Lady of Fatima shrine. When we walked into the lobby area, I had the feeling of being in a very beautiful, but not too austere monastery. There was regal furniture and old religious paintings surrounding us in the

∞

lobby area, with a wide, winding staircase to the rooms. I was looking for the elevator at this point, as I had just climbed a huge amount of steps to get into the lobby area.

I'm not sure if I was just tired from the climb, or if the desk clerk really was cranky. I was just anxious to get to our room and ditch the luggage, so we could get out there and see some things, before the darkness set in. We had used up a good bit of time in Santorum, but so glad we stopped there!

So, my friend opted for the stairs, while I loaded my bags onto the lift. As soon as the elevator door opened to the floor where our room was, the ungodly stench hit me like a freight train! My friend beat me to the floor and was ahead of me walking down the dark, meandering hallway. The odor seemed to get more horrific, the closer we got to our room. My friend had the key in the door, as I was catching up to her.

When she opened the door to our room, I

∞

was standing right in front of the door, kind of trying to catch my breath from the exertion. So the breaths I was taking were of the deep variety. I stopped dead in my tracks, as she swung open the door. I thought I was going to fall over! The unknown, horrific stench was emanating from our room. I could go no further, except to turn around and run out of that room, with all my bags in tow.

I was trying to get the words out, but my gag reflex kicked in and I felt like I was going to throw up right then and there. When I got back down the hall to where the elevator was, I managed to get my words out. I hoarsely said to my friend, who was not far behind me at this point, that there was no way I could tolerate staying in that room. She completely agreed, and guess felt a little sorry for my pathetic looking green gills.

She told me to sit down on the bench that was there, and she would go down to the desk and get another room for us. I complied and

∞

sat down and tried to get my stomach settled. I asked her to get a completely different floor, because that is how overpowering the stench was. It permeated the hallway of the entire floor. For such a sacred place, there was something very unholy about that smell!

We got settled in the new room, but the memory of that smell still lingered in my mind. It probably would forever. I found it to be really strange that the desk clerk did not even question the request for another room. We hurriedly unloaded the luggage and my friend wanted to go right out and tour the place. I told her I would meet up with her at the shrine in an hour or so, as I desperately felt the need to take a shower, just in case any of that stench got into my pores! So that is what we did. We parted ways for an hour or so. I took a long shower and scrubbed myself well.

The room was functionally adequate, not fancy, but beautifully austere, like a monastery. It did not have a bad smell

31

∞

except for a bit of mustiness from the old furniture. There were beautiful pictures of our Lady hanging over each bed. I again felt safe with her pictorial presence surrounding me. Through the window, I could make out the surrounding walls of the Grotto, where the Blessed Mother had appeared to the 3 children. I felt a deep peace come over me.

After my shower, and putting on clean, fresh clothes, I went to find my friend. She was there at the outside mass that was being said. I came into it at the middle, but stayed till the end. I was glad to receive the Eucharist and felt I was starting to settle down a bit.

It was such a beautiful ceremony, with the sun setting deep in the hills of Fatima, behind the altar. The hymns and praises were angelic and echoed through the mountainside, and the feeling amongst the people was one of incredible warmth. My friend decided to go back to our room to freshen up and then we were going to meet up and go to

∞

dinner before the 9:00 pm candlelight vigil. I decided to watch the mass from a bit of a distance, so I could stand awhile, instead of sitting on the concrete benches, as my back needed to do some stretching.

I was about 30 yards back from the outside mass, standing alone just watching the beauty of it all from a slight distance. I was enjoying this further out perspective of it all, with the Holy Mass and the sun sinking down into the glorious mountains behind it, when all of a sudden this woman approached me from almost out of nowhere. She began to converse with me. She asked me where I was from. I told her the U.S. and she looked into my eyes deeply and said the oddest thing.

She said, we pray for your country all the time in my country. I asked her where she was from and why she was praying for my country. She said she was from Canada, but did not seem to have a Canadian accent. I thanked her for praying for the U.S., but

∞

again asked her why and in what regard was she praying for us.

She said, because the U.S. seems to have their fingers in all the pots of the world, and there was a foreboding belief that because of this, we would continue to pay the dire consequences of war and retaliation. I thought about what she said for a moment, and knew she was right, and just thanked her again for her prayers and said good-bye.

It was almost dark now, and knowing my dysfunctional sense of direction, thought I should head back to the hotel. When I got there and went into our room, my friend was freshened up and I suggested that we go down to the small pub in the hotel to have a drink before dinner. She agreed and off we went.

When we walked into the little pub, located off to the side of the hotel's desk, there were a bunch of little tables and chairs and a bar. There were only two other people

∞

in there sitting at one of the tables and we took a seat at another table. I noticed there was no one behind the bar, and asked the couple if they knew if there was a bartender or waiter nearby. The female spoke up, and said, yes, that he would be right back. So, we started up a little conversation between the man and the woman couple. The two of them were sitting around a small laptop computer, that she had on the table in front of them. She was all excited and started to tell us about the little 'Fatima path' they had just come from. In fact, she invited us to come over and sit at their table to look at the pictures she had just taken and that were on her computer from that 'Path' they were on all day in the town of Fatima.

We got up to go over and join them at their table to look at their pictures, but I wasn't quite sure what I was looking at on her computer. She started to explain and point out the specifics in the pictures. There were 'orbs' of light, some surrounded by faces of people throughout the foliage on

∞

the 'Path.' It was astounding! I was looking at small children, some almost elflike, and others who were adults peeking from behind trees and bushes. She was so very excited telling us about it and saying we really must see it before we left Fatima, which was to be around 9 the next morning.

So my friend asked them how far away it was from where we were there at the hotel, and they both said a bit of a hike, but certainly within walking distance. Finally, the bartender appeared and I went up to order a glass of fine Portugal wine and my friend had hot chocolate. I could tell by the look on my friend's face, that she wanted to go and check it out right then and there.

It was now dark out and I had just sat down with my glass of wine and had no intention of doing any more walking at that point. I said to her that we would get up early in the morning and walk the 'Fatima Path', before we left for Barcelona. She said, that she just wanted to go to make sure we knew

∞

where it was, so to find it right away in the morning.

That she would be back in a short while and we would have dinner before the 'candlelight vigil' at the shrine. I said that I would wait there at the hotel for her, so off she ran.

Well, I finished my glass of wine and decided to go close by to see the interior shrine and get some pictures of that, while waiting for her. Well, I did that and was heading back to the room, when I got terribly lost. All the streets looked the same, as I trudged up and down hills. All the while the hotel was tucked away in a position where I could not see it, only a short distance away.

So I just meandered around street after street, stopping to ask locals where the Domus Pacis Hotel was? The problem was I did not know Portuguese and they did not know English. I continued my walk to find our hotel. I decided to walk in the center of

∞

the street to be able to get a better view of what was behind each side of the street, and it just felt safer to do that.

It was now very dark and Portugal had no real street lights in which to navigate up and down it's very steep, hilly streets. As I walked on, I noticed that there were very few people on the streets, but a persistent howling sound in the background, that seemed to be getting closer. I now walked more toward the center of the long winding, cobblestone streets of Fatima.

Suddenly, as I turned the corner, I came upon what appeared to be a pack of wild dogs. They were walking toward me and they now were stopped, looking directly at me. I stopped dead in my tracks and we just stared at each other.

I began to silently pray the rosary, which I had tucked in my jean jacket pocket. They didn't care much for me putting my hand in my pocket to hold the beads, and they again

∞

slowly walked toward me, with their heads lowered, barking, growling, and bearing sharp, glistening teeth, that seemed to light up the now dark night. My prayers picked up pace and I silently called upon St. Michael, the arch angel to please intervene, and right about now would be a good idea!

All of a sudden, out of the thick bushes to my right, appeared an old man, with some sort of cane or stick he had raised high into the air above him. He was quickly moving toward the pack in a threatening way. The wild dogs stopped their descent upon me and turned almost in unison to glare at this old gent heading straight toward them, ranting something in Portuguese. I could not understand what he was yelling, but more importantly, the dogs seemed to understand him quite well! They became all at once silent and turned around and walked down the dark, lonely street, this time away from me.

After I closely watched them depart,

∞

with my heart still pounding, I took a very deep breath and turned around to thank the old gentleman...There was NO ONE there and I immediately ran around the only corner he could have walked around, but the long, narrow street was empty! However, at the end of that long meandering street, I saw what appeared to be one of the spires that was atop our hotel. I ran as quickly as I could toward it, thanking God all the way up that hill.

Upon reaching the front of our hotel, a cab pulled up with my friend jumping out and yelling to me, have I got a story to tell you! I smiled and whispered to myself, and do I ever have one for you! We looked at each other and almost simultaneously said, let's go get something to eat.

With the stories we had to share at dinner, I had hoped we would not be late for the Candlelight Vigil. In the distance, you could see the brightening in the dark, night sky forming from the candlelight in the not

∞

so far off Fatima hills. It was a surreal site to behold! I would NOT miss this, for sure, even if I had to gulp my food down.

FATIMA (THE PATH)

We woke up quite early the next morning in Fatima, Portugal. We wanted to walk the Path of Fatima, as seen above, before we had to leave for our next part of the journey, to Barcelona, Spain. This was the same path where the children of Fatima encountered the apparitions of the Angel at Loca do Cabe.

Most textual sources describing the Fatima events mention only the Marian

∞

apparitions that occurred in 1917.

However, the girl Lucia Santos, the primary recipient of the apparitions, revealed some years later that three other apparitions in 1916, of a male figure, in fact preceded the Marian apparitions of 1917.

The story begins early in 1916 when the nine-year old Lucia was sent by her parents to tend the family's sheep in the hills near the village of Fatima. Her cousins Francisco Marto, aged eight, and his six-year old sister, Jacinta, accompanied her. The children were on a hillside when they saw a vision of a human figure. Later this beautifully luminous figure was referred to as an Angel.

After the wild night before, we still managed to get up early and go to the Fatima Path before we had to leave Fatima and head North to Spain. We had a very long day ahead of us, as we traveled from Portugal to Barcelona, Spain. We hit the Fatima Path at about 7:20 am and it was surreal!

∞

Because it was so early, we had the entire Path to ourselves. It was a beautiful, narrow path nestled in the little grove, high above the hills of Fatima, where the 3 children of Fatima had seen the Apparitions of the Angel in 1916.

As we stepped onto the Path, the sacredness of the moment and the stillness of the crisp morning air was palpable, or was it my heart thumping in the hollow of my chest that I was feeling? I stopped a brief moment, closed my eyes and prayed silently and tried to imagine how it must have felt for the 3 little children quietly tending their sheep, when a bright light had suddenly appeared before them. I tried to imagine how I would have felt. I fully understood why the first words from the Angel were 'fear not'.

∞

As we walked along the Path with the gnarly, low lying oak trees, the large, limestone Stations of the Cross were interspersed every 30 ft. or so to the right. When I peered to my left, I could see the early morning sun glistening upon the little town of Fatima. It was a breathtaking thing to see! A little further down the Path, between the Stations of the Cross, and to our right, a little higher into the hills, stood the huge, white stone statues of the Angel administering the Eucharist to the 3 kneeling

∞

children at the spot where Lucia had said it occurred.

I wanted to climb up and get closer. I wanted to stand on the earth, where they had been. I wanted to touch the rocks and feel the foliage. I wanted to experience what it must have been like with all my earthly senses. So, I began to climb up the rocks.

The feeling was exhilarating and I wanted to linger there a long time and feel that serenity for as long as I could. I would never forget that moment and the awe that it instilled in me. I knew I had to come down and move on, as there were still 5 more Stations to go and we had to get back and catch a train.

The consolation is that I can go back to that moment when I close my eyes and choose to do so. The Holy Spirit has emblazoned that into my mind's eye, so real, with even the very smells that were around me at that moment in time. It was a Blessing to leave with.

∞

CHAPTER III

LOURDES/ THE GROTTO AND THE BATHS

In the heart of the Pyrenees, Lourdes receives more than 5 million visitors from all over the world every year. As spiritually oriented as Lourdes is, I remember thinking how very commercialized it seemed to be with souvenir shops everywhere you looked.

On 09/29/12, we flew from Barcelona, Spain and arrived in Lourdes, France about 2 pm. We took a short cab trip in the gentle rain to our hotel in Lourdes. The Hotel Chapelle et Parc was a magnificent location on 28 Ave. Bernadette, right in the center of everything and it was popping with activity!

∞

Again being at the very foot of the Pyrenees Mountains, the streets were hilly and had side by side, little shops on both sides of the narrow street. I remember thinking how odd that automobiles were traveling up and down, dodging inattentive tourists everywhere.

∞

The Grotto is the sacred place where the Blessed Mother appeared to the devout peasant girl, Bernadette in Lourdes, France. The Blessed Virgin Mary appeared to St. Bernadette 18 times between Feb. 11th and July 16th 1858, when she was 14 years of age.

THE BATHS

To be honest, the decision to see and take part in this part of my journey was not easily made. It is not a pleasant experience, psychologically or physically. Although, spiritually, nothing else so far in my life has topped it!

There are 17 Baths in total: 11 for women and 6 for men. It entailed a good chunk of time, at least 2 hours standing in line. The physical look of the Baths are 2 low set buildings, one for men and one for women, that inside had several rows of benches separated by metal bars. Once you move to the interior of the open-air building, you sit

∞

on these benches and are queued along the maze like structure till you come up to the front of the queued line.

Then they place sets of 8 to 10 people on chairs right outside the interior entrance to the Baths, which were separated by a shower like, blue and white striped curtain. We recited the rosary as we moved along the maze of benches. It was quite beautiful, with each decade being said in a different language.

My heart raced the closer I got to the front of the line. I had no idea what was behind that shower-like curtain and my imagination was on overload! Once my friend and I walked behind that curtain, I began to realize my anxieties and why.

Ahead of me were about 6 more shower-like curtains with a lot of water pooled up in puddles on the unlevel masonry floor. It was my friend and my turn to go up to the final set of chairs before entering into the individual

∞

baths. I looked behind the chair where I was seated and noticed a row of hooks.

One of the helpers came toward me with a large, gray, wool blanket and stretched it out from arm to arm right in front of me. She then asked me to please stand up and take off my clothes and to hang them up on the hooks behind me. I swallowed hard and said, oh you mean down to my underwear right? She said everything off please.

Now, not only was it Oct. and quite chilly in the French mountains, but I was about to realize true vulnerability physically, emotionally and spiritually.

I felt tremendous humility in such a situation, but I slowly removed my clothes. The significance of that moment made me realize that this must be 'the way' we have to become before God, to really love and trust in Him completely. Not an easy task, I assure you!

Once completely naked, they wrapped

∞

me in a cold, damp towel and led me to the last curtain in front of me. As they pulled the curtain back, I gazed upon the marble bath, about 10' (l) by 5' (w), with 3 steps going down into about 3 feet of the natural spring water that Bernadette had discovered back in 1858.

I was instructed to say a silent prayer as I stepped down into the Bath, where upon reaching the bottom step into the Bath, I would be submerged. It was the very top step that skimmed the cold water that seemed to paralyze my body. My body immediately resisted going any further! It is important that I mention here that the temperature of that water was 50 degrees.

I whispered to myself to think of God only. Finally, my muscles began to relent and move slowly forward down the steps.

I was doing quite well, I thought, until I was immediately shocked back to the reality of the moment, once I felt the hands

∞

on my shoulders quickly submerge me into the frigid water. I let out a gasp and coming back up to the surface of the water again, I grasped the 10-inch statue of the Blessed Virgin Mary, that was attached to the front of the Bath.

All my emotions were released at that moment and I was shaking uncontrollably, as the tears flooded out of my eyes. As much as I tried, I could not repress them. I guess I was in there about 15 seconds and was then helped out and wrapped again in that wet towel and led back to my clothes that were hanging on the hook to get dressed.

I remember how quickly my body dried upon getting out of the water and going over to where my clothes were hung, without drying off with a dry towel. Again, the large gray wool blanket was raised around me to afford me some privacy while putting my clothes back on.

I felt an incredible sense of peace after

∞

coming out of that water! It's very hard to explain, but I was in a deep reflective state of mind. I guess I would describe it as close to a meditative state, however I wouldn't discount shock either! The water was extremely cold!

Once dressed, I immediately walked outside to wait for my friend. She came along not long after that, but looked kind of sad. I asked her what was wrong? She looked down at the ground and said, "I didn't do it." I just didn't do it….

I said well, don't feel so bad, cause that water was freezing cold! I knew she probably heard me gasp aloud as I entered into the Bath, and this had probably influenced her decision, and I felt bad. We split up for a little while and I went down to a little pub at the foot of the Pyrenees and ordered a glass of delicious Bordeaux. I wanted to be still for a while to watch the sun sink behind the beautiful mountains. I wanted to savor every moment!

∞

I sat there trying to take it all in, as I closed my eyes and prayed prayers of gratitude. I knew I would never in my life forget what just happened to me. I felt different. I felt reflective. I thought more about my sons and knew that Mary would protect them, but also knew it would take great faith!

As I sit here now writing this, it is 2 and one half years since I submerged in that Bath and prayed for my sons. Back then I surely did not understand just how much faith it would take to believe my sons would be safe. My youngest son today resides in Poland, which of course is next door to the Ukraine.

I began to cry again, just overwhelmed with the extent of what I had just experienced...

Damn, where is that garcon with my wine?

CHAPTER IV

BERNADETTE SOUBIROUS OF LOURDES:

THE EARLY YEARS

BORN: Jan. 07, 1844 DIED: Apr. 16, 1879

∞

Bernadette was the product of a marriage of love, that consisted of the two families, Casterot (her maternal relatives), who were master millers in Boly Mill, and the Soubirous family (paternal relatives), who were simple mill workers.

Francois, her father, loved Louise (her mother), in spite of the age difference between them. Her parents love for each other and their marriage flourished and endured in spite of many problems. It was a Christian family united in prayer, open to others, and full of charity towards those less fortunate then themselves.

There are two floors at the Boly Mill, where Bernadette first lived, the upper and the ground. The upper room is where she was born on Jan.7, 1844. She was baptized two days later, on Jan. 9, 1844, the day of her parent's wedding anniversary.

The ground floor was used for everything and served as both kitchen and living room.

∞

By day, it was a living room and by evening a place of prayer. This was the Mill as it was known to Bernadette, the Mill whose millstones turned in the flow of the Lapacca River.

The Boly Mill was named after its original owner. From 1844 to 1854, this was Bernadette's birthplace and home, a place of great happiness for Bernadette. She lived here with her parents, her brothers and sisters, and also with her grandmother, her uncles, aunts and cousins.

It was here, at Boly Mill, where Bernadette lived the first 10 years of her life in an atmosphere of love and faith. It was during these years, in this loving atmosphere, that Bernadette began to acquire qualities of personal strength and to develop a balanced temperament. These qualities would later help her to weather the storms of her life. The good times gave way to a period of hard struggle. 1853 saw the beginning of this difficult period.

∞

A number of issues merged to make life difficult for the family. For example, there came the industrial revolution with its introduction of steam mills, along with a great drought in the region. Also the family had a great generosity to the poor and were reluctant to force debtors to settle their accounts, all factors, which ultimately collapsed the family business.

Spring of 1854: the family could not pay their rent and were forced to move to a cheaper mill.

1855: A cholera epidemic soared through Lourdes, killing 38 people in 5 weeks. As a consequence of this epidemic Bernadette suffered chronic asthma for the rest of her life. In addition, the epidemic forced the Soubirous family to rent a cheaper mill, or face certain homelessness. This time they were forced to leave Lourdes and go to Arcizac.

1856: Master miller, Soubirous fell

∞

into bankruptcy, because when famine hit the area, the government distributed free flour. Bernadette's father was constantly looking for work, but often found himself unemployed.

Even though she had 4 children (2 having died very young), her mother was forced to go out and work. Bernadette herself worked for a little while at a local Inn where she was a waitress.

1857: The Family moved into the Cachot (the old jail). On March 27, 1857, her father, Francois Soubirous was wrongly accused of stealing a bag of flour and was put in jail for a week. So in order to decrease the number of mouths needing to be fed, Bernadette was sent as a housemaid to a farm in Bartres, where she minded the children and tended the sheep. She stayed in Bartres till Jan. of 1858.

1858... The Blessed Virgin Mary appeared eighteen times between February

∞

11 and July 16, 1858 near Lourdes, in southern France, when Bernadette was 14 years of age.

The Blessed Mother revealed herself as the Immaculate Conception, and asked that a chapel be built on the site of the vision, and told Bernadette to drink from a fountain in the grotto.

Feb. the 25th was the occurrence of her 9th Apparition. Bernadette heard the Lady say: "Would you mind going down on your knees…kissing the ground…eating the grass that is there for sinners? Go Drink at the Spring and Wash Yourself There."

No fountain was to be seen, but when Bernadette dug at a spot designated by the apparition, a spring began to flow. The water from this still flowing spring has shown remarkable healing power, though it contains no curative property that science can identify, but the many cures attributed to the Springs are indisputable by medical science.

∞

The One Room House of St. Bernadette

THE CACHOT...THE APPARITION

Cachot – a word which means jail or dungeon. It was a jail cell until 1824. This room which is the most squalid of the whole house was given free of charge to the Soubirous family, which was owned by their cousins as a refuge in a time of sheer desperation and hopelessness.

It is a single cold, dark room, where the Soubirous family stayed from June 1856 to autumn 1858, after the family's financial downfall. The furniture consisted of 2 rough beds and a single trunk for their linens.

∞

This environment had to be difficult for Bernadette to live in. Bernadette Soubirous, was about 12 years old, when her family of 7 moved to the Cachot. The eldest of five children of hard-working parents, she had suffered several childhood illnesses leaving her weak and asthmatic, and small for her age.

Bernadette set off from there to go to the Grotto, where she met the Virgin 18 times. From a very early age though, she showed signs of having immense faith in God.

Bernadette could hardly read or write, and she had great difficulty learning her Catechism, but was said to have whispered in a characteristic way that: 'At least she would always know how to love the good God.'

Of all the sites in and around Lourdes associated with Bernadette, the Cachot is probably the place, which has changed the least. The church of her baptism has been

∞

replaced; the Grotto has become the center and hub of a huge pilgrimage center (even the river Gave has been moved away from the place of the apparitions to provide a large arena for the crowds of pilgrims).

However, the Cachot, Bernadette's home, hidden behind towering shops and hotels, sits as it has ever done down a little side street, which is comparatively unchanged from its form 150 years ago.

Today after the renovations during the winter of 1995-96, still one can see all the bleakness of this room of 3.72m by 4.40m. which served at the same time as a kitchen, dining room, bedroom and a place of prayer for seven people. It is the property of the Sanctuary and visited by large crowds of pilgrims during the season. The Sisters of Charity of Nevers look after the building today.

In 2010, the Cachot was the most visited place in the Hautes-Pyrenees, with about

∞

300,000 visitors, according to the Department Center of Economic Development (CDDE).

This fact alone, made me realize just what a miracle it was for me to be alone in her home. In the early morning of Oct. 1, 2012, my friend and I ventured out to tour the city of Lourdes.

Our first stop was to be The Cachot. When we arrived there, I was taken back by the sheer image of the place. It looked very much like a prison; in fact, it resembled the

∞

prison I had worked at right after I graduated from college, the Bucks County Prison, in Doylestown, Pa., but only on a smaller scale.

As we approached this foreboding structure, I saw a man at the door. He was the fellow in charge of collecting the passes to get inside. He seemed like a very pleasant fellow. We gave him our tickets, exchanged some small talk and entered inside. As soon as we got into the room of the old building, my friend announced that she had to go to use the bathroom. Well, there were no bathroom facilities in there, so I said to her, well you go ahead, and I'll meet you back here.

I realized immediately after she left to find a bathroom, that I was the only person in there, and this was not an opportunity that I was willing to give up. That is to say, here I was in the busiest tourist place in Lourdes, and I was completely alone in St. Bernadette's house! I shook my head and smiled to myself.

∞

With camera in hand, I slowly perused around the dank room. I immediately felt the sacredness that was around me. I first saw Bernadette's bed by the window. I understand her parents placed her bed by the window due to her asthma. I remember immediately thinking to myself, what a damp, dark environment for one who suffered with asthma. However, I'm sure they were very grateful to be there and not on the street, which was their only other option at that time.

I next noticed how very lumpy her

∞

mattress looked, but was uplifted to see the view she had outside her window. In the morning she must have awakened to the sun coming up over the beautiful Pyrenees Mountains. At night I imagined how she could witness a celestial wonderland from her bed. This encouraged me, in spite of her most humble abode.

Clicking away, I was suddenly drawn to the empty fireplace in the room that was a combination of kitchen and living room. They had actually cooked all their meals in

∞

that fireplace. I envisioned how beautiful it must have looked when all aglow, and how that was their only source of heat! There was one solitary crucifix that hung on the concrete wall above it

Why was I so fascinated with this particular spot out of everything else in this little dungeon? I did not know, but took approximately 45 pictures of this fireplace from many different angles. Yes, I felt incredibly drawn to it indeed!

There was a large window to the left of the fireplace. In the middle of taking all these many pictures, I peered out of it. I was amazed to see a line of tourists that was almost wrapped around the block. At that very moment, literal chills went through my body and again tears filled my eyes, as I realized what an incredible blessing had just been bestowed upon me. To have this solitary chunk of time to be alone in this holy place. It was overwhelming!

∞

However, at that moment I really did not understand to what extent of a blessing it truly was! I would not know the power of it all until later on, as I was transferring my pictures from my camera to my computer.

Oh My God!!! My eyes were transfixed for what seemed like eternity on the monitor in front of me. Oh My God!!!

∞

Chapter V

The Final Days of St. Bernadette, Nevers, France

Bernadette decided to move away from Lourdes after the apparitions of our Blessed Mother. At the age of 22, she lived the rest of her short life as a nun and devoted her life to Mary. She spent many hours praying for the conversion of sinners, and to the service of God. Bernadette died on April 16, 1879, at the age of 36.

Her body was exhumed three separate times (1909, 1919, 1925) as part of a canonization process toward becoming a Saint in the eyes of the Catholic Church. Her

∞

body was pronounced as officially incorrupt (without rot) and moved to a crystal casket inside the Church of St. Gildard.

There is a minimal 'touching up' of the body, which is basically mummified with patches of mildew and calcium salts. The skin had disappeared in some places, but is still present on most parts of the body. Due to the darker color of her face, after death a light wax was applied over the skin of her face and hands.

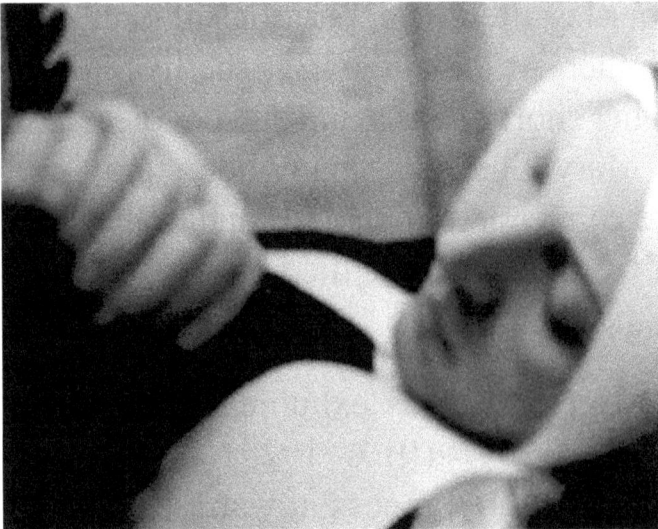

∞

On 10/03/2012, at 8:58 am we boarded a train from the Paris/Bercy train station and arrived in Nevers, France at 10:57 am, only a short 2-hour train ride from Paris. We booked a room for the night at the Hotel de Verdun, which was located at 4 Rue De Lourdes. It was a short 4-minute walk from our hotel to the incarnate body of St. Bernadette, which is on display at the Chapel of Saint Gildard at the Sisters of Charity in Nevers, France.

We dropped our bags off in the room and promptly left to walk to the Chapel of St. Gildard, where we would find St. Bernadette.

It seemed that this was a very hilly little town and I was just happy that we no longer had our bags to pull along behind us. As we ambled around the 2 blocks, I could begin to see the top of the chapel in the distance. Finally coming to the entrance to the courtyard of the Chapel, I realized it was beautifully ensconced behind a large masonry wall.

∞

Walking through the little gated entryway, I immediately saw the smaller replica of Our Lady of Lourdes to the left of me. Just like Lourdes, her statue was tucked into a small cavern in a tiny mountain enclave. Below and surrounding the base of her statue was a beautiful array of little votive candles that lit up her image in that dark tiny place.

In front of the candles there were several rows of small, old wooden benches, where one could sit and gaze at her serene but gorgeous face. I lit a couple of candles and sat there a little while in prayer and in order to give my friend some 'private' time alone in the chapel with St. Bernadette.

I got up from the bench and took the small walk across the tiny courtyard to enter the chapel. Instead of entering through the back doors, I opted to go in through the closer side door.

I opened that big wooden door and remember thinking how heavy it was. Well

∞

all thought processes came to a jarring halt, after I entered that dark little chapel. My 'thinking' just stopped. Everything stopped!

I did not at all expect to see what I saw. I remember blinking and trying to focus my eyes, thinking perhaps it would take my eyes a moment to focus while coming from the outside light into the darkened chapel. I was staring into the blessed face of St. Bernadette. The same face that looked upon my Blessed Mother, was right there in front of me, approximately 3-feet from behind the altar, where her body lay in a lit, crystal casket.

I could not move, and not thinking, allowed the heavy door to slam shut behind me. It bumped me forward a bit and knocked me back into awareness somewhat. The rest of the solace pilgrims in the quiet, little chapel turned in unison to look at me! Breaking through all kinds of silent meditation, I'm sure, geez! I silently mouthed the words, "I'm sorry."

∞

I slowly walked closer to her and knelt at the altar, not able to take my eyes off of her beautiful face! She looked like she was peacefully at sleep, certainly not dead! I was close enough to see her lower eyelashes and the tiny cleft in her nose. I was mesmerized! Here, in front of my very eyes was her beautiful being, that died over 130 years ago.

How could this be so? It made absolutely no logical sense to me on a scientific, rational basis. Then I quickly realized, of course it's not logical! What of God is perfectly, clearly logical in our limited human minds? After all, this was a miracle of God that I was witnessing.

The whole experience shook me, and when I think back on it, the very moment I first laid eyes on her, conscious thought really stopped and feelings took over. So I can't very well remember what my thoughts were, if any at that moment. However, it would be impossible to ever forget the

∞

pounding of my heart and the incredible peace that was upon me, as it will forever be burnt into my memory!

∞

CHAPTER VI

●❖●❖●❖●❖●❖●❖●❖●❖●❖●❖●❖●❖●❖●❖●❖●❖●❖●❖●❖●

JOURNEY TO ST. THERESE: LISIEUX, FRANCE

On October 2, 2012 we arrived at the train station at 10:24 am in Lisieux, France, which was about a 2 and one half hour ride

∞

from the Lazare train station in Paris. Again, we were tired and I felt bad because I kept my friend up half the night with my snoring. She was very forgiving.

As we rolled into the station at Lisieux, I remember how fast my heart was pounding! After all these many years, I was but a few miles away from my patron Saint, Therese... it was truly palpable and the French countryside was beyond words, beautiful!

We quickly retrieved our stuff and departed the train. We hobbled our 'stuff' toward the station. We hurried, because we were trying to get a glimpse of the departing trains to get back to Paris, so we could figure out how much time we had to see everything we wanted to see.

So, as my friend viewed the train schedule, I decided to go to the bathroom there at the station, so as to reduce this necessary distraction while at the Carmel convent of St. Therese. We were taking

∞

turns with our duties, so one could stay with the luggage, while the other took care of business.

Now France is different when it comes to public restrooms. You pay an amount to get into the stationary toilet, but when the door shuts behind you, there was no light in the room, and you have only a certain amount of time to do what you came to do, before the entire masonry floor was flooded with a rush of water. I suppose this was an attempt to thoroughly clean the area. I was kind of stunned when it first happened, thinking maybe a pipe had burst!

This was not easy to do, especially in the dark while crouching over a toilet. However, I somehow finished up and got back to my buddy (with very wet shoes), so she could take her turn.

As I was walking back toward her, I was looking down and taking my time, cause I didn't want to slip and fall with wet shoes

∞

in the middle of the Lisieux train station. I stopped dead in my tracks, as I realized I was walking on an area of the floor that was covered with red rose petals.

I yelled to my friend to come see this. We smiled at each other and I said, she (St. Therese) is expecting us. Was this just another little synchronicity that we encountered along the way? To say the very least, I was taken back at this moment and my heart jumped!

So, I sat there on the old wooden bench in the Lisieux train station while my friend went to use the bathroom. I just sat there looking at and wondering where on earth those rose petals came from. I suppose someone could have been running through the station with a bouquet of roses that had many petals drop from it, of course, that made sense to me.

I snapped out of my thoughts, and realized my friend was taking a very long

∞

time to come back from the bathroom. While distracted by the 'rose petals' that I was walking on, I remembered I had neglected to warn my friend of the strange bathroom.

I decided to walk across to the other end of the station to where the doors were that you went through to get to the bathroom. I made sure to keep my eyes on our luggage at the same time. I could not see her coming, so I went back over to get our bags. Grateful they were on wheels, I walked out to the bathroom door.

As I got closer, I could hear a pounding sound and a tiny, somewhat high pitched, frantic voice coming from the other side of the door. My friend had somehow gotten herself locked in there and because there was no light in there to be able to see where the lock was she could not get out. Of course, one could not open it from the outside if it was locked from within.

I could not help but laugh at the

∞

situation, but at the same time also realized the seriousness of it all. I yelled to her to 'hold on' and I would figure something out. I took our bags and walked back into the train station, where luckily I spotted a woman with a broom sweeping up the rose petals.

I walked over to her and asked if she might have a key to the bathroom, so we could rescue my friend. She quickly pulled a set of keys out of her pocket, and walked directly toward the bathroom. I looked down and scooped up the now neat pile of rose petals. I crammed them in my pocket, as I quickly followed behind her with our bags in tow.

It took only a second for her to unlock and open the bathroom door. There in front of me stood my very relieved friend. We laughed a lot, as we quickly took to the hilly road that led up to the Carmelite Convent/Church that stood in the distance. Our soggy shoes only slowed us down a little bit, as we

∞

giggled while trudging up the hill.

It was about three quarters of a mile up the long winding hill to the Carmalite Monastery of St. Therese. My heart pounded!

St. Therese lived out her final days on earth here. She was a Carmelite nun from 04/1888 to 09/1897. Lisieux is a quaint little village about 100 miles northwest of Paris in the Normandy section; a mere two and a half hour train ride from Paris.

We entered the Cathedral and went into the Chapel of the Reliquary. The church was beautiful beyond words! We came in through the back door and I could view an altar about 75 yards ahead of me.

On the altar in front of the crucifix, I could make out a small gilded, very ornate coffin. Actually it is called a Reliquary, as it contains some of the remains or first class relics of St. Therese. It is my understanding that it is the right arm of St. Therese.

∞

It is a belief that when people stand in the presence of her mortal remains or have some contact with her relics, God, who received through her humanity so many signs of love, is pleased in turn to manifest his love through her bodily remains.

I did not know about any of that, at the time, but I knew I had to touch that Reliquary. As my friend and I walked down the center aisle, there was some kind of prayer service going on in the front 10 or so pews. We slid into the first empty pew.

My friend whispered to me to go ahead up to the altar, where her remains were and she would snap a picture. Well, being raised in the Catholic tradition, I pondered a moment whether or not it might be rude to do so. However, it was not a Mass, so I went for it! I half expected to be stopped and disciplined on my way, but I hadn't come this far to be this close to her and not touch her casket. Besides, I had prayer requests I needed to deliver for friends. Off I went!

∞

It's not possible to relay the feeling I experienced when I put my hand on her casket! The only thing I remember was that 'tingling' feeling was back in my body!

It started with a very dull vibration in my legs (almost like a buzzing sensation) and shot up to the top of my head. I no longer cared about anyone's reaction.

I dropped my head and prayed to her. I reached into my jean jacket with my other hand and pulled out the prayer requests, and taking one small step to my left, dropped them into the basket next to her.

I did not want to take my hand off, but did so and returned to the pew where my friend was. She whispered to me that the flash had not gone off and wasn't sure if she got the picture.

Huh, really? Ok, I got out of the pew again, genuflected toward the altar and went back up. This time, I did so with a kind of determination and felt that it was a double

∞

honor to be able to touch it again.

I put my hand back on her casket and began to well up. I quickly said a prayer of thanksgiving and left to return to the pew. I felt like one blessed woman, and thankfully the flash worked that time! We quietly walked back down the long hill to the Lisieux train station to catch our train back to Paris. We didn't talk much, but our minds were full!

∞

CHAPTER VII

FINAL THOUGHTS

This spiritual journey was a highlight of my life. The experiences I had during these 10 days were nothing less than supernatural, in my opinion. I would describe them as more of visceral in nature, however no less real. Intellectually, I challenged them and at times considered maybe I was just tired and overwhelmed by the pace of the trip. Being in 3 Countries in 10 days via planes, cars and trains can do that to a traveler, no doubt.

But at the end of the day, there was really no way I could explain it all away due to fatigue. There are experiences I saw and

∞

felt and to this day, I have no explanation for them.

No real proof except for the picture I captured of the St. Bernadette apparition in the Cachot fireplace in her family home in Lourdes, France. I did not see this apparition (in person), so to speak, but only realized an incredible attraction that drew me to take many pictures of the fireplace in that one room house, that many called a dungeon.

There were many other items in that room that would have been far more interesting, but it was like I was mesmerized on this fireplace, that had one time been the place where St. Bernadette's meals were cooked and was it's only source of heat in the damp, dark and musty place. It had not been used for many years, but I was very drawn to it.

I chose to use it as the Cover of this book, however, as the title denotes, 'A Matter of Faith', it will have a different relevance for everyone.

^AMATTER ^{OF}FAITH

A Memoir of My Spiritual Journey
to the Marian Apparitions in Europe

∞

One of the biggest messages for me was the importance of maintaining faith, thus the title of this book. What is faith?

In the Bible, in Hebrews 11:1, there contains a clear definition of faith. "Now faith is the assurance of things hoped for, the conviction of things not seen." Simply put, the biblical definition of faith is "trusting in something you cannot explicitly prove."

The dictionary defines faith as "belief in, devotion to, or trust in somebody or something, especially without logical proof."

But as did St. Therese's', I believe it is true that our faith can falter at times, but because it is the gift of God, given to His children, He provides times of trial and testing in order to prove that our faith is real and to sharpen and strengthen it.

It has been my experience in life's many mysteries, that one does not always see what is there with our limited senses, however

∞

that does not automatically preclude that it is not real. There are countless stories accounted by many saying that they saw and spoke to a being, that when the scene was photographed, that Being was not there along with the other human beings in the picture. At other times, a Being is there on the scene, but not physically seen, but when the photo is taken, the Being is very much there in the picture.

In my situation, visually I saw nothing but an empty old fireplace. However, my other senses were highly alerted and I was drawn to take several pictures of it from many different angles.

I would almost explain it as a compelling urge! Also, in spite of the fireplace not being in use, there was a comforting warmth emanating from it in the otherwise cold, damp room.

After returning from the trip and putting all the pictures together somewhat in an

∞

orderly fashion, that is according to subject matter, I noticed something strange.

To make it clear, there was no kind of reflective material in front of the fireplace, so there is no chance of it being a reflection of something behind or in front of it. Besides, I was the only one in the room. When sorting through Bernadette's pictures, I put 2 of them next to the apparition in the fireplace and was astounded at what I believe are similarities.

∞

The first is a picture of St. Bernadette when she first became a nun.

The second picture is my picture of the apparition, I took in her home at the Cachot in the defunct fireplace.

This third is of St. Bernadette's incorrupt body at St. Gildard's Chapel in Nevers, France.

I make no official claim that who is in this apparition is St. Bernadette, because I have no proof. However, I know this apparition is St. Bernadette, because I have faith, and after all, isn't everything a matter of faith?

I'll let you decide!

About the

Author

Being of Irish/American descent and raised in the Catholic tradition, Kate Hoctor Bieler comes to this genre fairly naturally.

In her short writing career, she has taken hold of both the mystical and lyrical Celtic stereotypes in this, A Matter Of Faith, her feckless rendition of raw belief and in her past work of poetry, Under An Emotive Sky.

She has the realism and optimistic spirit of an American however, as she questions the world around her, while her God affirms it…

She will continue to seek and question that which is not always obvious, and put it out there for her readers to decide.

Stay tuned and enjoy her journeys...

Visit her website at:

http://spiritjourneymeauthor.com